K

The Inspirational Story of One of the Greatest Basketball Players of All Time!

Patrick Thompson

Introduction

This book gives an inside look at the life of Kobe Bryant, one of the greatest basketball players to ever graced the NBA.

Kobe lives and breathes basketball. While other basketball legends fade into obscurity after retirement, Kobe is out there pursuing new endeavors and building a business empire. It's a testament to his relentless thirst for knowledge and never-ending quest to be better.

This book is a front row ticket to Kobe's journey through life as he reveals how he used the Mamba Mentality as a blueprint to his success, whether on-court or off-court.

An insight into how his mind works offers an opportunity to replicate his success and achievements. It teaches about the value of hard work and commitment to the craft. Kobe's rise to greatness is an inspiration to a new generation of young people who dream of making it big in their chosen fields.

Thanks for downloading this book. I hope you enjoy it!

Chapter 1 Laying the Groundwork

Kobe Bean Bryant started playing basketball at the age of three, largely influenced by his father Joe, who had a stellar basketball career in the NBA and in the European leagues. His relationship with basketball is a love affair that ignited the moment he started shooting imaginary game-winning shots using balled-up socks.

At age six, Kobe knew that basketball was going to be his life and everything else would take a backseat. It was a natural progression for someone who had been exposed to basketball at an early age.

The Bryant family moved to Italy so that Joe could continue his basketball career after retiring from the NBA. Italian was his first language, but the language he speaks best is basketball. Although he was away from home, it didn't stop young Kobe from learning about basketball. He would watch videos of Joe's games and study them intently, learning every move.

Kobe also studied the games of athletes he admired the most. He would mimic the moves of Magic Johnson and Michael Jordan and pretend that he was a basketball superstar taking the buzzer-beater. He would be on the sidelines watching his father play and observing the nuances of the game that would become the love of his life.

But growing up in Italy meant that the lure of football was strong. It was almost like there was a pressure for every kid to play the sport. Coaches urged him to put his athletic abilities on the football field, which he did. Although he played football growing up, his passion and loyalty remained with basketball. He looked forward every summer because it meant going home to Philadelphia to play in the Sonny Hill League. Kobe was in his element when he played basketball. He relished every second of his time in the league.

When his father signed to play for a French team in 1991, the daily two-hour commute to his school in Switzerland took its toll on Kobe and his two sisters. It was a challenging and exhausting year for the family that a decision was made to move the kids back to the United States to continue their studies there.

When it became apparent that Joe's playing career was over, the family returned to Pennsylvania and Kobe's own basketball career started to take shape. With his talent and determination, Kobe made it to the basketball varsity team of the Lower Merion High School in Ardmore, Pennsylvania. The Aces made him a starter even though he was a freshman—a rare occurrence in the history of the team.

Despite the hard work, the team did not do well in the tournament. It was a huge setback for Kobe because all he wanted was for the team to win. He had developed a winning mindset early in his life that it was tough for him to lose. But he did not lose hope. Instead, he worked to change the team's mindset and dynamics. Flashes of leadership and brilliance made him a valuable player in the team's roster. Soon, the team started to play better.

Kobe's high school coach Gregg Downer remembered Kobe for his dedication to the game. He treated it like a battle zone and he was the fierce court general who rallied his team to victory. Even with a broken nose, he would play through the pain and just be a solid presence for his teammates.

It was not everyday that coaches would have a high school basketball player with such drive and maturity. Coach Downer ever had any doubt in his mind that Kobe would turn pro. In his senior year, he was scrimmaging with the likes of Jerry Stackhouse and Shawn Bradley and was holding his own against the two former NBA stalwarts.

Kobe developed a strong work ethic early in his high school basketball career because of his desire to win every game. To him, basketball was not just fun and games, it was a lifestyle. This kind of mindset endeared him to coaches and his teammates, but it was not always easy for him to socialize. Adjusting to the American teenage life was a huge challenge for him. He had a decent B-grade average, but academics was not the only thing that he had trouble with. Making friends didn't come easy. It's not because he was such a jerk in high school, but he's the type who gets too caught up with basketball that maintaining friendships is not really a priority.

Kobe's lack of friends stemmed from his childhood spent in Italy. His family kept moving from town to town or to wherever his father's contract took them. Fleeting friendships was the "normal" in Kobe's world. Always being the new kid town made it difficult for young Kobe to build a lasting friendship with other kids who had been together for a long time. It was too much effort to get into a clique only to be ostracized for being an outsider.

In high school, Kobe had the work ethic of a pro basketball player. He had no time for activities that don't contribute to his development as a player. He was too strict to a fault, but he didn't mind the criticisms because he had lofty ambitions. Some might find his attitude bordering on cocky and excessively self-assured, but he is just being himself and speaking the truth about the one thing that he can be arrogant about.

Kobe's unfiltered confidence may rub people the wrong way, but it's part of who he is as a basketball player and a person. His trash-talking can hit a nerve or two, but it was just part of the psych war to disrupt his rivals. He is just fearless on-court and off-court because he is confident in his abilities.

Even before the Mamba Mentality became his mantra, Kobe had already been putting it to practice during his high school basketball career. When he announced to the world that he was taking his talent to the NBA straight out of high school, it was met with criticisms and raised brows.

The pronouncement was loaded. In a way, Kobe was saying that he was ripe for the pro league and, at the same time, he was telling the world that he was too good for college basketball that skipping it was the right decision.

Kobe was not the first man to make the giant leap to the pro league, but he was the first one to announce it with such boldness and swagger. He was so self-assured that his skills and talent could compete with the NBA greats.

Many saw Kobe as an ambitious high school phenom who was fast-tracking his journey to the big league. What not many people know is that he had been preparing for his professional career since his junior year in high school. At that point in his life, he already had a strategy on how to make himself NBA-ready.

Kobe realized that the sure-fire way to get noticed by scouts, coaches and general managers was to be the best shooting guard in the roster. He started training as a guard and began improving his game. Coach Downer encouraged the kind of development that Kobe wanted to have because it fits his play style and his mindset. It didn't take long for mismatches to surface.

It became apparent that he was unguardable—almost invincible—in high school. It was not only good for his team, but it was also good for his ambition. The result was astounding: he averaged 31.1 points, 10.4 rebounds, and 5.2 assists per game. It was more than enough to land him the Pennsylvania Player of the Year. But the reality is that basketball is a team sport and no team can win solely on the brilliance of one player.

Even if Kobe carried the entire team to the state playoffs, his mind-blowing statistics were not enough to get the highly-coveted championship trophy. Their best was only good for a semi-finals loss to a better team.

Kobe got a dose of basketball reality. He was devastated but not broken. The experience only made him work even harder. The hunger to win never left him. He had a small window left to get the job done. The end result was an impressive run that delivered the first state championship title to the Lower Merion Aces in 53 years.

Every college in the United States was eager to sell its basketball program to Kobe. Duke, Michigan, Villanova, and North Carolina all jockeyed for position and waited for what could be their ticket to championship contention. While colleges waited with bated breath for Kobe to return their calls, Kobe set his eyes on the bigger prize—the NBA Draft.

Seeing Kevin Garnett getting drafted by the Minnesota Timberwolves right out of high school in 1995 gave Kobe the extra boost he needed to make his dream come true. With his sheer talent alone, Kobe had a huge advantage over other potential NBA draftees, but the fact that he worked with some players of the Philadelphia 76ers gave him an advantage.

Kobe's father struck a deal with the 76ers that allowed Kobe to scrimmage with the pros. It not only elevated his game, but it also allowed him to put his skills on display for coaches and scouts, which increased his chance of being drafted straight out of high school, just like Garnett.

In 1996, the high school basketball phenom entered the NBA Draft and was picked 13th by Charlotte Hornets. But even before Kobe could wear a Hornets jersey, Lakers General Manager Jerry West made sure that Kobe is shipped to Los Angeles in exchange for Vlad Divac. It made quite a stir in the basketball world.

Although Kobe's NBA drafting was a big news that reverberated throughout the sporting world, there was another story happening on the down-low that stole Kobe's thunder. With Divac out of the Lakers roster, there was enough salary cap space to sign Shaquille O'Neal who had just become a free agent after four years with the Orlando Magic. With the signing of Kobe and Shaq, West had laid the groundwork for the soon-to-be dynasty

Chapter 2 Work Ethic

Kobe's first game as a pro was forgettable: 0 points, 1 rebound, 1 steal, and 1 block in six minutes of playing time. His first career point came two days later against the New York Knicks. He looked nothing like the high school phenom that everyone was hyped about. But once he got his ball touches and shooting stride, he dominated the game.

Kobe's slow start in the NBA exposed him to criticisms mostly from detractors who were hell-bent on seeing him fail. Although his basketball skills are unquestionably great, his interpersonal skills leave a negative impression. He was smug, cocky, and swaggering. He didn't have the charisma of Shaquille O'Neal nor the magnetism of Michael Jordan.

Kobe is simply not personable—not in the way Jordan used his charm and personality to build his brand. Kobe never had the same level of popularity as Jordan outside of basketball because there was something about him that was inaccessible. Perhaps Kobe gave people reasons to hate him, but if there was one thing that everyone can agree on it's his strong work ethic. In that aspect, it's hard not to love the guy.

Never mind that his moves mimicked those of Jordan's, making him a carbon copy in terms of play style and basketball IQ. It's not uncommon for a younger player to imitate his idol's signature moves. It was also not a surprise that both Kobe and Jordan focused on winning.

What elevated Kobe to greatness is not his killer moves on the court, but it's his insane work ethics that stem from his competitive drive to outdo and outplay everyone. Kobe deserves the comparison with Jordan because he is the only one who had the same level of commitment to basketball and to winning.

Kobe's strict workout and practice regimen started during his high school days. While kids his age were still in bed, Kobe would show up to practice at 5 a.m. He would go on a two-hour shooting session and morning workouts until it was time to go to school. It was unheard of for a young kid and yet there he was acting like a professional player preparing for a playoffs game.

Kobe would challenge his high school teammates on one-on-one games to 100. None of them came close to beating him. On a bad day, Kobe would still win by a large margin without breaking a sweat. It doesn't matter if the teammate was a starter or a benchwarmer, Kobe would still take anyone head on.

When he turned pro, his workouts became more intense. His drive and motivation to win matched the level of commitment and the work he put in during practice. Not even injuries could stop him from practicing. Even with a cast on his right arm because of a broken wrist, he continued with his shooting session using his left hand.

Even NBA superstars Dwyane Wade and Chris Bosh witnessed the insane work ethic of Kobe. During the 2008 Olympics, the US team was just starting breakfast in the training camp when Kobe came out in his sweat-drenched workout gear. He had just finished a three-hour full workout while everyone else was still trying to shake the sleep off their system.

At times, Kobe would keep random players after practice so that he could try out new moves. He did this to bench-warmers or new players who don't get much playing time. Many people might look at it as a show of dominance on his teammates by making them guinea pigs. On the flip side, the players might look at is a learning experience from a future Hall of Famer. In any case, even Kobe's efforts for self-improvement involve other players in the team. It would be up to the affected players to rise to the challenge or make themselves feel inferior to a dominant force in basketball.

Anything that could improve his game or his physical condition, he would not think twice of pursuing it. In fact, he asked Nike to shave a few millimeters off the bottom of his shoes so that he could a better reaction time by a hundredth of a section. It would seem like it was just a negligible change—almost trivial—but he'll take it anyway because he believed that every tiny improvement can help him perform better on the court.

When it comes to fitness and health, he consistently made self-assessments to see if he needed to improve his weight or his nutrition. He was never been out of shape except for the times he was injured. He practiced precaution so that he doesn't get hurt. In preparation for the 2012 Olympics, he felt the need to shed 16 pounds because it would ease up pressure on his knees and make him in game shape by the time the Olympics season rolled in. He was always thinking of ways to improve his physical condition ahead of time.

Super intense workouts were always part of his daily physical regimen. The drills and repetitions alone can knock the wind out a regular person, but for a super athlete like Kobe, it was just part of the daily workout.

Kobe was also strict about what he puts in his mouth. Although he didn't take many supplements, he watched what he ate. He eliminated sugar and pizza from his diet and switched to lean meat

Some of the precautionary measures that he followed to prevent injuries were icing his injuries and doing acupuncture.

But injuries were pretty brutal to him in the later years of his career. His playstyle was so physical that the threat of a broken nose, an injured shoulder, or a sprained ankle always loomed in every game.

When Kobe injured his right shoulder, it didn't stop him from playing his A-game by using his left to get though the game. If it wasn't a serious injury, he would keep playing until the final buzzer sounded. But there was a time when he was reminded that despite his super athleticism, he is still human. When he tore his left Achilles heel, he still wanted to continue playing but the medical team stopped him from doing so because it could worsen and become a career-ending injury. It was out of his control and he had to follow medical protocol. But what was amazing was that he recovered so fast that he shattered the normal timetable for the recovery from such a major injury. It was as if he willed himself to get better.

Rehabilitation and recovery normally take nine to twelve months and even after the recovery, players who suffer the devastating injury are not immediately allowed to play. If they are given the go-ahead, they only have a limited playing time. Achilles injuries affect players over 30 years old the worst. Kobe was 34 when he suffered the injury. He was past his prime but he was still dominating the court with a 46 percent shooting average. Even so, the threat of not being able to get back to his pre-injury peak was high. It was potentially a career-shortening injury at the least and career-ending at the most.

After Kobe recovered from the injury, he never quite got back to the game shape he was in before the injury, but his statistics were nothing to sneeze at. He still played the hardest and the most intense games of his life until he decided that it was time to retire in 2016. In his last game as an NBA player, he destroyed the defense and dominated in the offense, scoring 60 points to defeat Utah Jazz. It was a storybook finish for a colorful NBA career.

Because of his winning mindset and strict training routine, not many players can keep up with his energy. While his teammates were cruising, Kobe was on overdrive. Some of his teammates recognized his deep commitment to winning, but they didn't fully subscribe to his methods.

Kobe hates laziness. He felt that some players were not putting in enough work to win and he wasn't afraid to voice out his opinion regarding the matter. He would scold his teammates for celebrating an overtime win knowing full well that they played crappy basketball. He could not tolerate mediocrity because he has always conditioned his mind and body to win.

Naturally, his obsession with winning rubbed his teammates the wrong way because he could be overly critical of his teammates. NBA All-Star Dwight Howard knew this all too well during his short-lived stint with the Lakers. Kobe and Howard never got along because one is the polar opposite of the other. Howard was not comfortable with the locker room culture that Kobe created. It made him uncomfortable because he preferred a more laid-back approach to the game.

The Lakers locker room under Kobe's leadership is anything but laid-back. Kobe created an environment where players are picked apart every game. It was a necessary ritual to keep everyone on the same page. Kobe wanted to win and he was teaching his teammates how to achieve that ultimate goal. The locker room reality made Howard uncomfortable and he could not deal with that kind of environment. In the end, Howard was dealt to the Houston Rockets where he was able to shine.

To Kobe's credit, many of his teammates subscribed to his approach because they have a common goal and want to win an NBA championship ring before they retire. It was evident that the in-your-face confrontational and combative method worked for Kobe, but it was not for everyone. It was not for softies and cupcakes—it was for players who are tough enough to take the criticisms and work on their weaknesses.

And then there was Shaq. If there was one player that frustrated Kobe the most, it was Shaquille O'Neal. While Kobe's training intensity was always on high gear, Shaq is at sloth's pace. Shaq was known for coming to training camp overweight and out of shape. It was a far cry from Kobe's physical and mental condition. The stark contrast in their physical conditions says so much about the level of commitment that Kobe had and the lack of discipline Shaq had.

Shaq's laziness to keep in shape drove Kobe crazy. It added to the personality clash that they had going on as soon as they became teammates. Shaq's work ethic ran contrary to what Kobe was inculcating to their teammates. It was a source of frustration and disappointment for Kobe because it was affecting their title run in the early 2000s.

To his credit, Shaq would shed pounds during the season by playing himself to game shape. However, this was not acceptable to Kobe. It wasn't enough effort and it made him question Shaq's commitment to the team and to the team's goal.

No one really knew how much excess weight Shaq was carrying and he would sidestep the issue every time the press brought it up in interviews. The problem was that even though

Shaq was well aware of his weight problem, he did not make efforts to slim down to be more effective in his game.

Kobe, who did crazy things just to get even the tiniest improvement in his efficiency, saw how Shaq's problem can be a team problem. Even though Shaq still dominated the paint with his sheer size and strength, his effectiveness diminished in direct proportion to the increase in his overall body weight.

Had Shaq been more disciplined and stayed fit, he would most likely have helped extend the Lakers' winning streak with Kobe and perhaps added more championships to their belts. This is the same "what-if" that drove Kobe insane. Kobe knew things could have been better had Shaq been more disciplined and more in sync with Kobe's fitness routine.

It is not difficult for Kobe to find players who have the winning mindset. Most players have the same goal in the NBA, and that is to win championships. However, the hard part for Kobe is finding someone who has the same intensity and passion for basketball as he does. This made it more difficult for the Lakers management to find another big name to pair up with Kobe.

Kobe's cutthroat drive can be likened to Michael Jordan's but Kobe had more swagger and arrogance that rubbed people the wrong way. He was too sure of himself that he could carry a team on his back even when there were other stars in the team.

There's no one else in the NBA that had his intensity and obsession—that is until LeBron James entered the picture. What not many people know is that LeBron adapted Kobe's physical and mental conditioning approach. Kobe was LeBron's motivation to keep getting better and that says so much about how effective Kobe's methods are. But not every player is driven or disciplined enough to do the work. Only those who do can be rewarded by a ring or two or three—just ask LeBron.

Chapter 3 Mamba Mentality

At face value, the Mamba Mentality may appear to be a brilliant marketing tool to elevate the Kobe Bryant brand. It's largely true if one has to look at it from the business side of things. But to Kobe, it's a philosophy that pushed him to do great things, not just in basketball, but also in other aspects of his life. It's the blueprint to which he elevated his game to get the best possible outcome—win multiple championship rings.

The Mamba Mentality is the mentality that enables a person to constantly become the best version of himself/herself. It's a mindset of continuous improvement. It is the legacy that he wanted to leave to the younger generations so that they can achieve their goals and dreams. It emphasizes on the never-ending quest for answers to questions that could improve one's self. It promotes the mentality of infinite curiosity. It is not hinged on other people's opinions.

Other variables that do not contribute to one's improvement are just noise that can be disregarded. The focus is on being in the moment and constantly improving, no matter how small the progression is. As long as you emerge better than you were yesterday, there's no need to worry about the end result.

The Mamba Mentality is what defined Kobe's colorful 20-year career in the NBA and it continues to characterize his attitude and approach towards self-improvement beyond basketball. It promotes the mindset of always performing at a high level and giving a hundred percent maximum effort. Nothing is wasted when you know that you gave your all in what you do.

Not many people realize the significance of the Mamba Mentality to the success of the Los Angeles Lakers during its title run with Kobe at the helm. It's easy to attribute the success to Shaq because he was such a beast on the court. His presence and dominance outshone Kobe. It was expected because Kobe was still trying to find his way and his role in the team back then. Shaq was the face of the franchise and Kobe had to play the second fiddle. But because of Kobe's Mamba Mentality, he was not intimidated by Shaq nor was he affected by the negative comments about him.

It was easy to hate Kobe because his self-confidence was seen as a display of arrogance and conceit. His play style was described as showboating and selfish. Odds were stacked against him when he was still a rookie trying to make a name for himself away from the huge shadow cast by Shaq.

The first half of his career, when he was still wearing the No. 8 jersey, was all about growing up and learning the ropes. Even then, he showed flashes of brilliance, but his greatness had not yet fully emerged. He worked hard every day not to please his critics, but to keep improving his game. He didn't let the negativity affect his game. He was focused on getting better. The result was an explosive and fearless Kobe who was instrumental in the Lakers championship titles for three consecutive years in 2000, 2001, and 2002. He had made his stripes and he finally got the recognition that he deserved. But more than that, he had silenced his detractors who didn't believe in his ability to win championships.

At the start of the 2006-2007 NBA season, he began to wear No. 24. To spectators and other players, it was nothing more than just a change in jersey number. However, to Kobe, it had a bigger significance. Although Kobe is still Kobe whether he was wearing No. 8 or No. 24, he admitted that he had a different mentality when he donned No. 24.

Kobe explained that the era of No. 8 was all about proving to himself and everyone else that he belonged in the NBA. It can be remembered that his first two games were unimpressive and lackluster. No. 8 was all about aggressiveness and energy. Kobe was hell-bent on showing what he can do on the court. It was about getting individual accolades and pushing one's limit to build a basketball resume worthy of fan-worship. He proved that his Mamba Mentality can win championships as long as players are committed to doing the work. He made it look easy—but convincing his teammates to subscribe to the philosophy was anything but easy.

When Shaq was traded in 2004, it became clear that Kobe was going to be the leader of the pack. He switched to No. 24 in 2006 as a symbol of growth and maturity. It was the end of an amazing era as No. 8.

Kobe had already racked up experience and championship rings that he really did not have to prove anything to anyone. But Kobe is not the type to rest on his laurels. He had a new role to play and he wanted to be a better version of himself—even better than what everyone thought was the "peak" Kobe.

In 2006, Kobe was already 28 years old and one of the older guys in the Lakers roster. He was no longer the young gun who razzled and dazzled the crowd. He was the picture of growth and maturity. The physical attributes were not the way they used to be. With a decade of playing with intensity and fierceness, something had to give. The injuries he sustained did not stop him or slow him down from chasing rings, but they have their impact on him physically.

Outside of basketball, he was also starting a family of his own. With marriage and kids, his attention was divided. He also had to take care of the business of marketing his brand. He had a lot on his plate and he had to play different roles. The obsession with basketball was still there and his loyalty to the game he loves never faltered. But he knew that he had to take on a different role in the Lakers team.

Shaq's absence was felt and Kobe knew that he had to step up if the team wanted a repeat of their title run. It was a more difficult challenge leading the team and trying to fill the gap that Shaq left. Whoever was going to take his place had massive shoes to fill—literally and figuratively. It turned out that none of the centers they had in the roster going into the 2005-2006 season can fill the void. It put more pressure on Kobe. Without Shaq, the team would have to work even harder if they wanted to be in title contention.

The change to No. 24 was symbolically a clean slate for Kobe. The feud he had with Shaq spilled over the locker room and created a toxic environment. Although Shaq's absence was sorely missed, Kobe knew that the team had to move on and re-align their focus and goals.

Through that challenging point in his career, Kobe had to trust that the Mamba Mentality could help him weather the storm as he transitioned into a new role. The honeymoon was over and it was time to get back to work.

While No. 8 was all about making his presence felt in the league and racking up crazy statistics, No. 24 was about reinventing and solidifying his career. It was a renaissance of sorts for Kobe.

Kobe learned to be a leader by watching how the legends play—Larry Bird, Magic Johnson, and Michael Jordan. It was what he needed to make the team come together and work to achieve their ultimate goal.

The second half of his 20-year career was better than everyone thought it would be. Kobe averaged 29.3 points per game, became an MVP, made it to his 10th All-Star, and led the Lakers to back-to-back titles. His mentality shifted to be in sync with his new role as a leader and facilitator—but more than that he became the heart and soul of the Los Angeles Lakers.

Because of his deep commitment to basketball, he created the mentality to size up opponents and beat them. It was not just about learning their tendencies and habits on the court, it was also about obsessively searching for any weakness that they have. It became second nature to know opponents at their very core until he knows them like the back of his hand. The more he knew about his opponents, the more ammunition he had in his arsenal. But this time, he wasn't alone. His teammates have learned to embrace the Mamba Mentality and used it to improve their game.

Kobe admitted that he obsessed about the equally explosive Allen Iverson. They were rivals on the court and they try to outplay each other. There was a time when Iverson put 41 points and 10 assists on Kobe in a Philadelphia 76ers home court. Players tend to play well and score big in their home court. The cheers of the crowd had always been a morale booster for the players.

No one was surprised when Iverson outscored and outplayed Kobe. It was expected and it came with the territory. But Kobe took it as his failure to do his job. He didn't care about factors like home-court advantage, luck, or breaks of the game; all he cared was that he was outplayed and he had to avenge the embarrassment. He didn't care what other people said about his game; all he cared about was how Iverson's stellar performance made him feel. He knew he failed at the one thing he had set out to do—he failed to stop Iverson from scoring.

Because of Kobe's mentality about winning and losing, he knew that for someone like Iverson, it was not enough to just work hard and hope for the best. He needed to do more. So, he studied Iverson obsessively in order to learn every weakness and every struggle. He watched tapes of Iverson's games dating back to his high school years. He also read every article he could find about Iverson. He wanted to dissect the man to know his state of mind. He wanted to figure Iverson out so he could be always two steps ahead.

The next time Kobe and Iverson met was a little over a year after the previous one. Iverson had the upper-hand by virtue of the homecourt advantage in Philadelphia. Iverson had 16 points at half time. Coach Phil Jackson only gave Kobe the assignment to guard Iverson on the second half. The game ended with Iverson stuck at 16 points. Kobe held him scoreless for the entire second half of the game. Revenge was sweet for Kobe. It was the Mamba Mentality at work.

Even though he succeeded in frustrating Iverson, he didn't like how he made him feel in the first place. Kobe didn't want his actions to be controlled by someone; he wanted the freedom to choose who he wanted to target. If someone or something compromises his future goals, then that's the time he would react and obsessively hunt down the perpetrator. He didn't want other things to get in the way of his goals and dreams.

Chapter 4 Basketball Muses

It's no secret that Kobe idolized Michael Jordan. He practically copied some of Jordan's signature moves. He added some Kobe touches here and there and made them his own, but the basics came from Jordan. He got every move and mannerism down pat. If one has to watch Kobe and Jordan in one screen simultaneously, the moves would be almost identical. Some critics used this as conversation fodder, especially in "GOAT" discussions. They said that Kobe can never be the GOAT because he's just a copycat.

Kobe acknowledged the similarity in play style and moves. He never denied imitating Jordan. In fact, he admitted to watching and studying Jordan's moves while he was growing up in Italy. When he returned to the United States, it became evident that he was not going to grow an inch taller than 6'6", so he began to study Jordan's moves obsessively and almost exclusively.

Jordan made a significant impact on Kobe's life. When Kobe entered the NBA and started matching up against Jordan, he was surprised at how open Jordan was to having a mentor relationship with him. Jordan's willingness to take him under his wings was something that Kobe could not forget. He considered himself lucky and privileged to have been the recipient of advice, strategies, game plans, and workout regimens from one of the basketball greats to have ever lived.

Jordan's influence on Kobe's career as a player is evident in the way he attacks the baskets or reads opposing players. But more than that, Kobe learned about leadership through Jordan. When he took over the leadership role after Shaq left the Lakers, Kobe turned to the lessons he learned from Jordan. As a result,

Kobe became a mentor himself, teaching former Lakers young guns like D'Angelo Russel, Julius, Randle, and Jordan Clarkson.

Kobe is also fortunate to learn from Lakers legend Magic Johnson. He had guided Kobe in different stages of his career. Magic was particularly helpful when Kobe sustained a potentially career-ending injury that sidelined him for months. Magic helped him gain perspective. It was the first time in his life that he understood and accepted the finality of his basketball career. He knew that his playing career would not be there forever, but the reality only hit him when he tore his Achilles heel. With help from Magic, he gained a new perspective and started to have a positive outlook in life even if the end was on the horizon. He learned to understand and appreciate the situation which made things less difficult to accept.

This is why Kobe keeps telling rising basketball stars to look to the legends for guidance if they want to succeed in their respective careers—the same way he did when he was still the arrogant player who thought he knew everything.

Chapter 5 Feuds and Controversies

Shaq

An explosive personality with a stubborn streak is bound to clash with other strong personalities when something big is at stake. Kobe had figured in several feuds mostly involving his Los Angeles Lakers teammates; the most infamous of which is the one he had with Shaquille O'Neal.

Kobe and Shaq played together for eight years from 1996 to 2004. Not even three championship rings could extinguish the animosity between the two. They had since patch things up and openly talked about their beef in a TNT sit-down special. Still, it was a feud that added intrigue to the Los Angeles Lakers' narrative as they mounted their title run campaign in the early 2000s.

Kobe and Shaq fought a lot about many things—from team roles to shot selections to contracts to getting in shape to team leadership. When Shaq signed with the Lakers during his free agency, everyone knew that he would be the leader of the team. On the same year, the Charlotte Hornets drafted Kobe and immediately sent him to the Lakers. It was clear who was the top dog in the team and it wasn't Kobe. He wasn't even number two because he had not proven himself in the pro league yet. His debut didn't even live up to expectations.

The feud started with something as petty as jersey sales and then had a life of its own and escalated into a dumpster fire that not even Coach Phil Jackson could stop. Apparently, in 1998, Kobe's popularity was on the rise and his jersey sales were outpacing Shaq's. Shaq then accused Kobe of playing selfish basketball and for showboating.

It didn't help that Lakes general manager at that time, Jerry West, criticized Shaq for "hazing" Bryant. This was further exacerbated when then Lakers coach Del Harris designed the Laker offense around Bryant during a playoffs game against the Utah Jazz. The result was embarrassing to say the least—Kobe shot, not one, but four air balls, in an overtime loss. Shaq, who fouled out with still two minutes in the regulation, was angered by the early playoff exit because he knew he would be blamed for it.

The beef intensified in the 2000-2001 season when Shaq showed up in camp overweight and out of shape. It drove Kobe crazy because he knew that it will affect their game negatively, especially when Shaq is the go-to guy in the post. Kobe demanded for a change in play and wanted the offense to go through him. Shaq didn't want to relinquish his role and wanted the ball to run through him in the post. Coach Phil Jackson called them both juvenile for fighting.

Although there was still bickering at the start of 2001-2002 season, Shaq and Kobe played nice throughout the season resulting in their third championship in three years. The ceasefire was short-lived because things got heated once again in the 2002-2003 season. This time, it was Shaq fanning the flame when he dropped the "company time" line when he refused to get toe surgery in the pre-season so he could play sooner. He reasoned that he got hurt during company time so he'd rehab on company time as well. This soured his relationship with the Lakers management. In his absence, Kobe stepped up his game and became more aggressive leading the team into 13-game winning streak. Despite Kobe's stellar performance, the team bowed to the eventual champions San Antonio Spurs. The Lakers' championship run ended with a sour note.

The 2003-2004 was a dark time for the Lakers team. Kobe was accused of rape during the summer and his status with the team was uncertain as he faced legal battles. At the behest of Shaq, the team signed Karl Malone and Gary Payton to add to the offensive firepower. Shaq started to ignore Kobe and kept leaving him out of the conversation. In an interview, he said that the team was complete even though it was evident that Kobe was at the training camp. Shaq vowed to keep in shape for his teammates but did not include Kobe.

The barbs in the press got out of control up to the point where Phil Jackson had to intervene to prevent a full-blown press war between the two superstars. Kobe had threatened to fire back at Shaq if he kept saying things to the press. Everyone thought that they would hear the end of it, but when Kobe returned to training camp, things escalated. Shaq continued to criticize Kobe's selfish gameplay. He said that he voiced his opinions because he was the leader of the team. Shaq even told Kobe to just opt-out of his contract because Shaq was not going anywhere.

As promised, Kobe fired back at Shaq in an interview with ESPN. He was relentless in his statements and criticisms against Shaq, telling everyone that Shaq was fat and out of shape and yet he blamed everyone in the team for the team's failure to advance to the Finals in the previous season. He criticized Shaq for exaggerating his injuries to cover up for his poor game condition. He also brought up the issue of Shaq lobbying for a contract extension while two veteran superstars were practically playing for peanuts.

Teammate Brian Shaw tried to intervene but only made it worse because he reprimanded Shaq when he yelled "Pay Me" at owner Jerry Buss after dunking in a preseason game. Furthermore, when Kobe complained about his teammates' lack of support during the most difficult time of his life, Shaw said that Kobe had never made efforts to build relationships outside the confines of the basketball court.

Shaq, to his credit, promised Malone and Payton that he would stop attacking Kobe in light of the rape charge against him. It was the start of the de-escalation of the feud. During the season opener, Kobe and Shaq decided to put the ugly feud behind them and focus on winning championships again.

Although the feuding had stopped, the controversy and the intrigue surrounding the Lakers did not stop. While the team was off to a great start with a 21-3 record, trouble was brewing regarding contracts. Owner Jerry Buss was not keen on giving Shaq a three-year extension with a $30 million salary increase. The Lakers management was hoping that Shaq would agree to re-sign for less money because of his age, deteriorating physical condition due to injuries, and poor conditioning. What made things worse was that Buss was unwilling to double Phil Jackson's salary to $12 million. Kobe's free agency after the season also added to the Lakers' mounting manpower strife. It was reported that Kobe was in serious talks with the Los Angeles Clippers.

When Jackson's contract was not renewed, there were speculations that Kobe had a hand in the decision because he had been unhappy with Jackson's offensive plays. Buss echoed Kobe's sentiments and said the he wanted to bring back the fast-break offense that that Showtime Lakers were known for. Jackson also expressed his displeasure with Kobe by saying that he wouldn't want to return to the Lakers if Kobe re-signed with the team.

Shaq immediately demanded to be traded after learning about Jackson's departure from the organization and upon hearing general manager Mitch Kupchak say that he would consider trading Shaq if necessary. Shaq believed that the decisions were made to placate Kobe and to build a team around him. Shaq didn't want to be part of a team where he would play second fiddle to Kobe.

The decision to trade Shaq to the Miami Heat was then made. The Lakers got Caron Butler, Lamar Odom, Brian Grant and a first-rounder in the next NBA draft. The end of the Shaq era in Los Angeles ushered in the Kobe-led Lakers who have a lot to prove with the absence of a big man and a brilliant coach.

Coach Phil Jackson

Kobe's feud with Jackson was low-key and was largely eclipsed by his long-standing feud with Shaq. More often than not, the animosity was hidden in carefully worded statements and clever answers to interviews. The two have already mended their relationship but Jackson had revealed details of their spat in his books.

Jackson didn't hide the fact that trying to get Kobe to play by his rules was difficult. With three championships together, it would seem that Kobe executed designed plays but Jackson alluded to something on the contrary. Jackson criticized Kobe for always going off the edge and showing off how good he was. When he found out that Jordan was watching in the stands, Kobe put on a show and scored 40 points in the first half.

Jackson also said that Jordan was more coachable than Kobe. He added that Jordan was more willing to take his advice than Kobe. This said a lot about Kobe's attitude towards Jackson's coaching and how he regarded himself. It made Kobe difficult to work with or play with. Kobe's extreme competitiveness was sometimes a bane to the offense when everyone was playing well.

Kobe's "irrepressible fire" made him too aggressive. His drive doesn't always match the drive of his teammates so he was always critical of them when they were not playing with the same intensity as he did. He was relentless and impatient. Jackson said that even though Kobe and Jordan were similar in many ways, Jordan had a conscience. Everytime Jordan became too aggressive offensively, Jackson would take him out of the game. Jordan would get back to the court and adjust his game. Kobe, on the other hand, would insist he be put back in the game to score more points.

Jackson also said that at times, he felt Kobe's hatred. Kobe had said in the past that he disliked Jackson and his coaching style. They never really got along the way Jackson got along with Jordan. The problem was that Kobe wanted more freedom to create plays, while Jackson wanted him to be more disciplined and follow his rules.

To avoid more friction, Jackson gave Kobe a license to do his thing as long as it meshes with the triangle offense that Jackson was known for. Since they have a common goal, they agreed to compromise. It is unlikely that Kobe really hated Jackson with a passion, but they were always at odds with each other when it comes to the kind of offense that they want to execute.

It was easy to pacify Kobe—as long as he had the ball, he would not complain. Kobe and Jackson's relationship improved when O'Neal was traded to the Miami Heat. Kobe had more control of the ball and he had more freedom to create plays within the framework of the triangle offense. The result of the compromise is two more championship rings, post-Shaq. There's nothing like championship rings to change the mood in the locker room.

Lakers Teammates

Shaq was not the only one Kobe butted heads with—Chris Mihm, Kwame Brown, Smush Parker, Brian Cook, Andrew Bynum, and Dwight Howard were all at the receiving end of the Black Mamba's overly critical lashing.

The Lakers' 2005-2006 roster can be considered lacking in talent and a complete mismatch to Kobe's drive and winning mentality. When a gifted player with a high basketball IQ and an obsession for winning plays alongside a bunch players with average skills and just cruising along, it's a disaster in the making.

In 2012, Kobe did not hold back when he said that Smush Parker was the worst guard in the NBA and didn't deserve to be in the league. He added that the only reason Parker was in the roster was because the Lakers management was too cheap to sign a competent point guard. Kobe didn't even want Parker talking to him during practice. Up to this day, Parker is still waiting for Kobe to apologize for the vitriolic attack.

Kobe also didn't have nice words for Chris Mihm. When Kobe was criticized for taking at least 45 shots per game, he shot back and said, "What was I supposed to do? Pass to Chris Mihm?" There was nothing subtle about his backhanded remark. He not only did he not have confidence in Mihm, he also belittled his skills and efforts.

Kobe had no love for former No. 1 draft pick Kwame Brown, too, but with good reason. During Brown's last game with the Lakers, he told Kobe not to pass him the ball even if he was open because he was nervous and that if he got fouled, he would miss the free throws. It made him appear weak and unworthy of the $7 million that the Philadelphia 76ers offered him.

The barrage of criticisms did not stop with Brown. Andrew Bynum was part of a four-team trade that allowed Lakers to get Dwight Howard. Kobe simply ignored the departure of Bynum whom he played with for seven years. He went as far as to say that the Lakers got Howard for next to nothing, alluding to Bynum being of little worth. His scathing remarks dealt a big blow to the receiver, after which the relationship became irreparable.

Dwight Howard played laidback basketball. He was not used to the strict locker room dynamics where Kobe was free to criticize his teammates and point out what everyone was doing wrong. Kobe tried to teach Howard how to develop a championship mindset, but Howard preferred to be his own person.

Howard thought that Kobe held the ball too much and it affected other players' offensive game. Howard tried to downplay his feud with Kobe saying that it was created by the media because there was nothing to talk about when the Lakers didn't advance to the Finals.

After a two-year stint with the Lakers, Howard landed in Houston. It would seem that there was a business to settle when the two got involved in a scuffle during a Lakers vs. Rockets game. Howard elbowed Kobe square on the chin while trying to protect the ball after a rebound. Harsh words were exchanged and a flagrant foul was called on Howard. In the end, Howard and the Rockets gave the Lakers a beating.

Ray Allen

Kobe and Ray Allen were in the same draft class and had a similar career progression until Kobe rose to superstardom and reached iconic status. In 2004, when Allen was still in his prime and playing for the now-disbanded Seattle Supersonics, he criticized Kobe Bryant for playing selfish basketball. He added that Kobe was scoring massive points every game so he can prove to the NBA and to the fans that he is better without Shaq and can with championships without him.

Allen even went so far as to say that Kobe needed two and a half good players for Lakers to become a legitimate playoff contender. He predicted that if Kobe does not win a championship in two years, he will go ask Buss to trade him. The trade demand happened but never materialized.

As expected, Kobe didn't take the criticisms too well and told Allen that he would bust his ass. He added that Allen was not in the same league as him so his name should not be uttered in the same breath. That was how fiery Kobe was.

Despite getting the ire of the great Kobe, Allen knew he was right. As predicted, Kobe struggled to carry a team with no stars for three years. The second title run was dead before it even started. Kobe may not acknowledge Allen's uncanny prediction, but it haunted him for years. When they faced each other in the 2008 NBA Finals, the Lakers vs. Celtics rivalry was re-ignited. Kobe didn't bust Allen's ass, but the Celtics gave the Lakers a proper ass-whooping.

The Chicago Bulls Trade "What-If?"

Ray Allen's prediction was spot on and no one was giving him any credit. It was true that Kobe was selfish and he carried the Lakers team on his back. But what no one expected was Kobe's trade demand. He was already in discussions with the Chicago Bull before the Lakers dealt Shaq to the Miami Heat. It was true that Kobe couldn't save the talent-less Lakers and as Allen predicted, he wanted to be traded. The trade didn't happen because the Lakers could not afford to lose both Shaq and Kobe in the same year.

Rape Accusations

In 2003, Kobe was embroiled in a scandal that could have ended his career and destroyed his legacy. A 19-year old woman came forward and accused Kobe of raping her at the Lodge & Spa at Cordillera in Colorado where Kobe was recovering from his knee surgery. Fans were in disbelief, the entire NBA was in disbelief, and Kobe, himself, was in disbelief. His defense was that they had consensual sex. It was a he-said-she-said situation, but clearly, because of Kobe's stature, he had the upper-hand. When the woman's name was leaked to the public, she refused to testify in the trial. As a result, the charges were dropped and Kobe dodged a bullet that could have killed his career and ruined his life.

In a civil suit, both parties agreed to a settlement, the details of which were kept under wraps. Part of the deal was for Kobe to issue an apology. In the apology, Kobe admitted that a sexual act took place, but he reiterated that he believed it was consensual. He said that he recognized that the woman did not view the incident the same way he did. He understood that the woman did not consent to the sexual encounter. It was telling of the dark side of Kobe Bryant—that he cheated on his wife Vanessa and that he used his power to take advantage of a woman.

Kobe could have gotten a harsh sentence; instead, he got a slap on the wrist. He went on with his life as if nothing happened. He won two more championship rings and secured his legacy. The sexual assault charges did not have any substantial impact on his career. If there was one aspect of his life that was massively affected, it was his endorsement deals. Some of his big backers were quick to drop him because they didn't want the negative publicity—especially when the crime is as heinous as rape.

McDonald's severed all ties with Kobe for good. The family-friendly fast food giant could not afford to be associated with a celebrity who was already marked as an alleged rapist, even though Kobe was not really convicted of the crime.

Ferrero SpA dropped Kobe immediately after learning of the allegations and did not renew his contract with Nutella. The company didn't want to besmirch its image by having Kobe's face in its marketing campaign.

Other companies waited with bated breath for further developments in the case before making a decision. Coca-Cola let Kobe's Sprite deal expire because renewing it could impact the image of the product, which was marketed to younger kids. But since the company was not yet ready to ditch Kobe, they signed him as an endorser for Vitaminwater, which is operated by an independent unit of Coca-Cola.

Spalding didn't see the need to ditch Kobe because the case didn't put a dent to their sales of Kobe basketballs. The company felt that it did not warrant ending the endorsement deal prematurely.

Nike was the only company who fully supported Kobe. The company stood by him and even used the negative publicity to create the Black Mamba personality that represented the dangerous side of Kobe. It was more than just a clever marketing move because it allowed Kobe to be more upfront to the public about the side of him that is largely misunderstood.

It would appear that corporate America can easily look past Kobe's past transgressions because years after the settlement, Lenovo and Turkish Airlines even inked deals with Kobe. In fact, Kobe earned over $20 million in endorsement deals in 2013—not a bad deal considering Kobe's image has already been tainted.

Even if all of Kobe's sponsors turned their back on him, he would still be okay because he had signed a very cushy $136 million contract with the Los Angeles Lakers and he could get more if he remained healthy and kept playing.

***

Kobe's feuds stemmed from the very nature of his personality. It was something that came packaged with his physical and mental gifts. He didn't ask to be at odds with his teammates or his rivals, it just happened because he held himself to a high standard and it spilled over to his expectations of people he played with. So, when his teammates kept disappointing him with their mediocrity, it was just natural for him to lash out at them. It was not meant to denigrate them nor to make himself appear superior, but it was meant to motivate them to do better and be on the same page. They wanted to be champions but they were not willing to the work; much less work as hard as Kobe did.

When the Lakers management shipped Shaq to the Miami Heat, they failed to surround Kobe with players with the same winning mindset. So, Kobe took upon himself to try and teach them how to be like him in terms of developing the mentality that would drive them to championship contention. However, they never rose to the challenge because they were not willing to do the work. Shaq may have been lazy, but he was physically gifted and mentally strong. He could keep up with Kobe even if he was lazy and laidback. It wasn't' the case for the others that's why there was friction everytime Kobe tried to intervene and dictate what each player should do. His methods were divisive because he was imposing something that was beyond the capabilities of his teammates.

The Lakers found a remedy in 2009 and 2010 when they built a competent roster that willingly subscribed to Kobe's methods and did the work. The result was two championship rings that were more meaningful than the three that came before them. Kobe proved to himself and to the world that he could win a title without Shaq. It took a while to convince his teammates, but it was worth the wait.

***

In light of the #MeToo movement, Kobe's rape case resurfaced in discussions, especially when he won an Academy Award for *Dear Basketball*. Although the award was in recognition of his artistic and creative works, the public is not willing to separate the artist from the alleged rapist. In fact, Kobe was banned entry into the Academy of Motion Picture Arts and Sciences, despite winning an Oscar.

According to the Academy by-laws, individuals who win an Academy Award are nominated for inclusion in the organization, which now has over 8,000 members. Kobe was already voted to be included, but the Academy governors committee overruled the affirmation, citing that Kobe must first show evidence of a larger body of work. Although it was the official stance of the Academy, it was also a diplomatic way to pacify those who demanded that Kobe be stripped off of his Academy Award.

Kobe revealed that he didn't know what the outcome would be had he not figured things out for himself. He had limited options: let the situation swallow him or figure something out. He knew he was bound to find a solution because he obsessed about it. He wanted to know how to overcome a huge problem that was bound to follow him wherever he goes. When he allowed himself to be honest and truthful, he knew that people will stand by him. Kobe had weathered the storm and is thriving in his second career.

Chapter 6 The Storyteller

When Kobe retired in 2016, no one knew exactly what his next steps would be. Sure, he had business ventures and the Kobe Bryant brand was still as strong as it ever was, but everyone wanted to know if his next effort would still be within the basketball world. The natural progression was to coach a team or mentor players as an assistant coach. He could also be a consultant or even a team owner—he knew how to lead, so owning one wouldn't be a far-off idea.

Little did everyone know that the 5-time NBA champion has a knack for storytelling. Before he retired from pro basketball, Kobe wrote the heart-felt and painfully honest poem *Dear Basketball.* The poem had an impact because it was Kobe's raw emotions captured in words. It was moving and showed Kobe's love and passion for basketball.

The poem marked his official retirement in 2016. It wasn't the last we've seen the poem. Kobe turned the poem into a 5-minute animated short with the help of animator Glen Keane and composer John Williams. By recruiting two industry heavyweights, the animated short was turned into a masterpiece worthy of critical acclaim and an Oscars nod.

The animated short premiered at the Tribeca Film Festival. Kobe even performed it live with Williams conducting the orchestra at the Hollywood Bowl. His newfound career as a storyteller created Granity Studios. He coined the word "Granity" from the phrase "greater than infinity." The studio is devoted to creating and developing stories that would be shared with the public.

Retirement did not slow Kobe down; not one bit. The second act of his career involved his role as CEO of Kobe Inc.

He is also a general partner of Bryant Stibel, which is a $100 million investment fund for media entertainment startups such as Scopely and The Players Tribune, among other startups.

Kobe's goal is to create timeless stories that can inspire people and make them become better versions of themselves—pretty much what Mamba Mentality is trying to instill in people who are willing to embrace the philosophy and the way of life.

It was an unlikely path for his second career but it's something that he's currently thriving at. When he won the Oscar for Best Animated Short Film at the Academy Awards, Kobe had something that no other NBA player has ever achieved. He can truly say that he is a cut above the rest with his achievement in his new venture.

What not many people know is that Kobe has always loved stories—reading them and plotting them. He has always been fascinated by how characters develop as the story progresses. He is particularly interested in stories about hard work and dedication. He is inspired by stories where the characters defy the odds and achieve success.

One thing that motivates Kobe to tell stories is that he wants to see how people react to them. In particular, he wants to see the reaction from kids after reading the stories. He's curious about how children interpret the symbols and meanings and if they are able to gain something from them.

Kobe made no secret that he and his family are huge Harry Potter fans. They are so invested in the stories and they geek out. He is also blown away by Game of Thrones. His passion for reading laid the groundwork for the new ventures he has outside of basketball.

Even before his retirement, Kobe had already produced a TV documentary called *Kobe's Bryant's Muse*, which is about himself, his career, and the people that inspired him. He wanted to tell his story but mostly about the things that he was comfortable talking about. Directed by Gotham Chopra, the documentary painted Kobe as a wounded warrior who was uncertain if he can still bounce back after a potentially career-ending injury.

Kobe's creative endeavors have been non-stop ever since the success of *Dear Basketball*. He released his non-fiction book aptly titled *The Mamba Mentality*, where he shares his knowledge about the game he loved and teaches how to play basketball with heart and passion. It was no surprise that it became a bestseller—it's Kobe's life told in pictures. It's accessible and relatable even though the man is one of the basketball gods that kids with hoop dreams look up to. It is for this reason that much of his creative projects are geared towards children and young adults. He wanted to inspire kids to chase their dreams no matter what their circumstances are.

The Punies is one project that was made for children. It is a scripted podcast about kids having a great time playing sports. But it's not always fun and games, because the kids also have to deal with a lot of things that come with growing up. Their relationships with one another develop and grow as they play the sports they love. Kobe created the show because he wanted to show kids that they can have fun playing sports and at the same time they learn how to deal with life's challenges as they interact with one another. He wanted the kids to develop a sense of responsibility and discipline at a young age so that they can thrive in the real world as adults.

The Academy Award nod for his animated short truly gave him a boost and the confidence to keep making stories that could inspire a new generation of readers and content consumers. With the help of staff writers and editors, his ideas are transformed into something concrete which can be shared to everyone. Three young adult novels are in the works and two more are scheduled for release in 2020. With his own animation studio and publishing house, Kobe can very well become a prolific storyteller.

Kobe also produced *Detail* for ESPN under his Granity Studios. He hosts the first season where he analyses and breaks down plays so that viewers can have a better understanding of basketball.

Kobe envisions infinite possibilities. Everywhere he looks, he sees potential stories. He believes that everyone has something festering within and it needs just the right push to turn it into something tangible. He is teeming with ideas because he is interested in so many things.

While others are okay with just accepting things as they are, Kobe's inquisitiveness knows no boundaries. He is not satisfied with just second-hand information; he goes straight to the source. For instance, when he wanted to learn about building a studio, he consulted Oprah Winfrey because he knew that he could valuable insights not available elsewhere.

When he wanted to understand characterization and getting into character, he turned to Award-winning actress Hilary Swank. When he wanted to understand world-building in stories, he picked George R.R. Martin's brain about building a universe. He learned the tricks of the trade from the authorities in their respective fields.

Not many people have the opportunity to do what Kobe had done. It shows how serious he is in learning new things and putting the Black Mamba spin to every learning that he has acquired. It's one of the reasons he has succeeded in his new endeavors thus far.

Chapter 7 Kobe, Inc.

When Kobe ended his NBA career in 2016, he went out with a bang. His 60-point outburst in his last game with the Utah Jazz was the perfect ending to a colorful career in basketball. He loved basketball with all his heart and if he could play forever, he would. Mentally and spiritually, he still has more than enough gas in the tank, but physically, his body has had enough. He knew that he could never defy Father Time.

When he took the floor at the Staples Center, he thanked the fans, the players, and everyone who supported his career. He ended his speech with the catchphrase "Mamba out!" On that very same night, "Mamba out" T-shirts were being sold on Kobe's official website. To many people, it was a clever marketing move to profit from the retirement—a last hurrah from the business of playing basketball. But to Kobe, it was a perfect transition to his next ventures in the world of business.

Kobe is no stranger to business. Because of his NBA career, he was able to build the Kobe Bryant brand. His net worth is over $600 million and it didn't all come from just playing basketball. He is a smart guy who did his homework before investing money on various business ventures.

The Mamba Mentality works in business as well and Kobe profited massively from it. Of course, the name Kobe Bryant has a lot to do with his success in other fields of interest. It's a powerful brand that attracted big names and even bigger investors.

Even with a strong brand, Kobe didn't rely on other people to do the work. He is a very hands-on entrepreneur who didn't stop asking questions. His never-ending curiosity and thirst for knowledge are paramount in his decision-making.

At first, his curiosities were limited to basketball and sports. He was focused on learning Michael Jordan's deadly fadeaway shot and Hakeem Olajuwon's lethal "Dream Shake". But his interests expanded to other things that have always festered inside of him. He has the habit of cold-calling people—famous and influential people—because he wants to learn more than what was seen on the surface. He cold-called legendary composer John Williams and invited him to lunch because he wanted to know how Williams builds crescendos into his masterpieces. He did the same with to other influential celebrities including Anna Wintour of Vogue. If ordinary people would do what he does, they would be shot down at the first opportunity. But he is Kobe Bryant and he could get away with it.

Perhaps his obsession with learning stemmed from his lack of education. In a way, he could be overcompensating for not earning a higher education in the traditional sense. He learned the practical side and the application of theories by simply being naturally inquisitive. Everything he does is deliberate. He made his intentions known and he had no ulterior motive but to learn. From the lessons he learned, he slowly but surely laid the groundwork for his business empire.

Kobe teamed up with Jeff Stible and created Bryant Stibel, a venture capital firm with a $100 million fund focused on technology startups, entertainment media, and data companies. They hit the ground running by making investments in much-publicized startups including juicing company Juicero, sports media website The Players Tribune, and legal service provider LegalZoom. It was a bold move for someone who was still earning his stripe in the realm of business.

Professional athletes tend to go the traditional path when it comes to their investment and they normally steer clear of ventures that bring more uncertainty than profit. But Kobe is known for taking risks because he believed in his abilities. Just two decades ago, there was a kid who announced to the world that he was taking his talents to the NBA because he was too good for college basketball. Cocky as it may have sounded, it was a high-risk investment where the product is himself. He was just replicating what he did 20 years ago, but this time in a venture capital setting.

Kobe believed in the products he invested in because they have a high potential to become profitable for years to come. Unfortunately, not all products live up to their potential and fall short of expectations. Juicero failed and folded because its juicer was overdesigned and overpriced. Most of all, it was inconvenient and complicated to use. The controversy that surrounded the fancy juicer was the reason for Juicero's downfall.

It was a minor setback for Kobe, but a setback, nonetheless. The upside is that most of the business ventures of Bryant Stibel are still standing and thriving. Not bad for someone who's just testing the capital venture waters.

Things started to look up when Kobe's $6 million investment in BodyArmor returned a massive financial windfall of $200 million. It was not too long ago when Kobe had the wherewithal to invest in an upstart sports drink that claims to have more potassium and less sodium than the leading sports drink. BodyArmor also has coconut water, which is one of its biggest come-ons.

Kobe recognized that from a standpoint of innovation, the sports drink category has been dormant for a long time. People have become so accustomed to consuming only one brand of sports drink because it was the only one available to them. There was a monopoly of some sort because a giant beverage company is pushing it to sports teams across leagues. Kobe saw the potential of BodyArmor because it is an upgrade to what people are used to drinking. It also helped that the sports drink is being endorsed by super athletes like Rob Gronkowski, Andrew Luck, Buster Posey, and Mike Trout.

Kobe became the third largest shareholder behind the two founders, Michael Repole and Lance Collins. Repole and Collins both sold their respective beverage products to Coca-Cola before banding together to create BodyArmor.

It proved to be a smart investment move for Kobe. When he made his first investment in BodyArmor, it made a decent $10 million in sales. When Coca-Cola entered the scene and invested in BodyArmor, Kobe's stake in the company ballooned to $200 million, which accounted for a major chunk of his estimated net worth. But more than that, BodyArmor is set to compete head-on with Gatorade, the leading sports drink owned by Pepsi. With Kobe's involvement in a huge business rivalry, he had tasted a different kind of success outside of his basketball career and he wanted more.

There's no sign of stopping Kobe from making his presence felt in the business world. His latest idea became tangible when he released Art of Sport (AOS), the performance-driven line of body care products that took almost two years to develop. The brand offers essential products targeted at athletes and active individuals. His knowledge about athletes and performance helped inform the products' botanical rich formulas. Deodorant, soap bars, body wash, and sunscreen are the first line of products introduced in the market.

During the R&D process, Kobe decided that he wanted to partner with top athletes and action sports champions to promote the brand. NBA MVP James Harden, MLB All-Star Javier Baez, and NFL Star receiver Juju Smith-Schuster signed up as partners. AOS is the fusion of Kobe's passion for sports, business, and high-performance. The opportunity for growth is high and Kobe is already thinking of expanding the product line.

When Kobe embraced his new role as a businessman, his efforts to learn about the wheeling and dealing in business turned into an obsession—the same obsession he had for basketball. He's putting in serious hours in his business just like he did when he was still playing pro basketball. He's constantly texting and taking calls left and right. He's obsessively monitoring the performance of his investments and making sure that he's always on top of things. He's working while the rest of the world is sleeping. Nothing much has changed, the same wiring is still there, there's just a different focus.

Kobe's obsession stems from his nature to care for something he is passionate about. He doesn't rest until he's satisfied with the outcome. He can't just sit and wait for his investments to grow or fail, he felt the need to get involved in every aspect of the business process. Even though there are competent people that run his businesses and investments, He didn't want to be just a figurehead or an endorser; he wants to be a hands-on entrepreneur.

When Kobe attended the National Association of Convenience Stores conference, he was there not as an endorser of BodyArmor, but a business owner who spoke about why the sports drink is different. He believed in the product and he preached about it like a minister at the pulpit. He's extremely confident that BodyArmor will takeover Gatorade as the number one sports drink by the year 2025. When asked why he was very optimistic about the product, he said that when he was still a kid, many people kept telling him his odds for making it to the NBA—the odds were far worse than BodyArmor's.

He had graduated from the picture-taking and autograph-signing Kobe to empire-building Kobe. He has arrived in the business and his responsibilities run deeper and the stakes are much higher because there are so many moving parts involved. His decisions do not only affect himself but other people as well.

Building a business empire is hard but making sure it does not collapse is even harder. Those who know Kobe are not worried about failing. Nike Chairman and CEO Mark Parker recognized that Kobe is just as intense on-court as he is off-court. To Kobe's credit, he changed the basketball shoe game in 2008 when he demanded low-cut basketball sneakers. It proved to be what the consumers wanted. The low top sneakers were a huge success that Nike would not think twice about collaborating with him again. Kobe may be a pain in the butt when it comes to business ideas—he had millions of them—but the final outcome has always been positive.

What Kobe learned from industry stalwarts was that at the core of their business is love for what they do. It's the same factor that pushes him to do better at his job. One of the lessons he learned and took to heart is that he can enrich himself within by making other people's lives better. It's not always about the product, but the people that are working to improve the product.

It's clear that Kobe wants to dominate the business world the same way he dominated basketball, and with the way things are rolling, Kobe may just surpass his on-court success—and it's a scary thought for his rivals in business.

Chapter 8 The Future

Kobe had just entered the land of the big 4-0. He's having the time of his life; after all, life begins at 40. He churns out ideas faster than he can dribble the ball and if his current projects are any indication, he'd be creating massive content for his Granity Studios.

Kobe made it clear that his creative storytelling is not just for entertainment; it is a multimedia vehicle that can help athletes maximize their talents and live up to their full potential. He has already given the public a taste of this unique content in *Detail* for ESPN, where he gives an in-depth analysis of basketball plays and recommends improvements to the game. With his expertise, he could have a solid career as a basketball analyst or commentator. He's also opened to mentoring the new generation of NBA players. He's often giving out his opinions and observations about their play style and offering suggestions on how to improve them. For instance, he's been very upfront about Ben Simmon's lack of jump shot and James Harden's volume shooting.

Even though retired from playing, Kobe never really retired from basketball. He's still involved in the sport in different capacities. Apart from content creation and storytelling, Kobe's is looking to educating a new generation of children through sports. The MAMBA Sports Academy is just the start of making his commitment to empowering kids a reality. The Academy is a holistic multi-sport training facility in Thousand Oaks, California especially designed for young athletes. It also has an eSports training ground and a Jiu-Jitsu school in partnership with Gracie Barra. The principles of the Mamba Mentality will be infused into the teaching program to help young athletes develop a winning mindset and a strong commitment to high level of performance.

Kobe's burgeoning businesses will always keep him busy, but never too busy for his philanthropic projects. With the Kobe & Vanessa Bryant Family Foundation, the Bryants are providing financial support and resources to kids, young adults, and families worldwide. Through the Foundation, unique programs are developed to improve communities so they grow and become self-reliant.

Kobe's retirement allows him to spend more time with his family, especially now that they are expecting their fourth *mambacita*. With his second daughter Gianna hell-bent on playing for the University of Connecticut, Kobe will have his hands full juggling different roles.

Now that Kobe is no longer chasing championship rings and no longer out proving to the world how great he is, he can focus on new ventures that can have a positive impact on people and the community. Kobe has come a long way from being the cocky and arrogant high school basketball phenom to a basketball icon that inspired generations of kids. Kobe's basketball legacy is already secured, but the Black Mamba is just starting to build his empire.

Chapter 9 Life-Changing Lessons from the Black Mamba

1.   **Find your passion and you'll never have to work a day in your life.**

Basketball has always been Kobe's passion. It was not just a sport that he played; it was his life. It consumed him and he obsessed about it. He studied the all-time greats and learned from them. His commitment to basketball is unparalleled. Before he got drafted in the NBA, he was already primed for professional play. He practiced hard every single day to improve his craft. Many professional players are too lazy to practice because they consider it as work. To Kobe, he finds pure enjoyment in working hard because it is where his passion lies. When he's on the court, it never felt like work.

1.   **There is more than one way to achieve a goal.**

Winning is Kobe's goal whenever he is on the court. But no matter how prepared he is, there are other variables at play that is beyond his control. For instance, winning is not just about making shots; it also requires great defense. When things don't go according to plan, coaches and players must adjust and find another way to win. It's the same with life. There are stops, starts, and restarts because not all plans turn out to be good ideas. Always look for alternative routes to success when the main road is congested.

1.   **Don't be afraid to ask for help.**

Early in Kobe's career, he came across as arrogant and egotistic. Many adjudged him as self-absorbed and conceited. What not many people realize is that he never really relied on his knowledge and skills. He knew early on that he needed help to improve his game. He was not satisfied with his stats and he knew there was lacking in his game.

Self-absorbed people would not seek help because they think of themselves as superior to everyone else. Kobe sought advice from the likes of Michael Jordan, Hakeem Olajuwon, Magic Johnson, and Jerry West. He knew that he'll get valuable advice from experts that could help improve certain aspects of his game. He didn't think twice of calling the coaching staff and the medical staff when he had questions about his physical conditioning. The more he asked for help, the more he learned something new.

1. Use negative feedback as motivation.

When there is negative chatter around, Kobe always appears unaffected. This is not because he is devoid of emotion, but because he knows how to handle the criticisms. Instead of letting the scathing remarks affect his game, he used them as motivation to do better. The negativity becomes an opportunity to make adjustments in life. Not many people have the ability to turn something negative into something positive, but Kobe thrived when there are negative criticisms about him because he used it as a motivation.

1. Failure is an opportunity to try again and do better.

Kobe's debut as an NBA player was laughable. He was scoreless and spent most of 48 minutes sitting on the bench. This was the high school phenom that was touted as the second coming of Michael Jordan, but all they saw was a potential bust. He never got his rhythm in his first few outings. He shot one air ball after another. He had no chemistry with his older teammates and his execution was tentative. It was a performance not worthy of play time. With Kobe's mentality, he used his early failures as learning tools to improve himself. He watched games and studied them intently until he identified the areas that he needed to focus on. The next time he entered the court, he made it impossible for the coaching staff to take him out because he was playing so well. Failure is temporary if you work on your weaknesses and strive to do better.

1. Keep moving forward.

By the age of 30, Kobe had already won championship rings, received the Most Valuable Player award, and got an Olympic gold medal. People didn't expect him to perform at a high level all the time because they think that there was nothing else to chase. But Kobe is always hungry for more. He didn't rest on his laurels because he wanted to test his limits. Most of all, he wanted to prove that he could win championships without Shaq, just to silence the people who created the narrative that he only won titles on the strength of Shaq.

Even in his retirement, Kobe kept exploring and finding ways to improve himself. He ventured into business and tapped into his overflowing creativity to build something that can impact lives. He keeps moving forward and reinventing himself.

1. Success requires commitment.

To Kobe, success is more than just a goal; it's a way of life. His commitment to success is unmatched by his teammates and contemporaries. He developed a kind of discipline that allowed him to be in his best physical shape. His mental toughness enabled him to remain focused even when things don't go according to plan. He created a system that makes it difficult for him to fail. It is not fool-proof, but the Mamba blueprint has proven itself five times over.

1. Setbacks provide opportunities to re-evaluate

Losing in the 2004 NBA Finals against the Detroit Pistons was a big blow to the Lakers. They were defeated convincingly by the underdogs who had no superstars in their roster. It was a monumental setback for Kobe, who was quick to take the blame for the loss. There was no upside to losing, but it gave Kobe the opportunity to re-evaluate himself and the team. At that time, the Pistons frustrated Kobe by not allowing him to get many ball touches and when he did have the ball, his shots would not fall. With the opportunity to re-evaluate comes the adjustments to the game and overall attitude. This also happened in the Lakers loss to the Boston Celtics in 2008. They got everything wrong in the finals that year, but they made major adjustments in 2009 and 2010, which resulted in back-to-back titles.

1. The most adaptable trumps the strongest and the fastest.

In the first few years of his career, Kobe was an intense showboat. It was all about aggressiveness and energy. Fancy dunks, deep threes, and fadeaway shots rounded up his repertoire. He was criticized for his poor shot selections and selfish one-on-one plays. He realized that his flamboyance on court was not sustainable and had no place in a championship contending team. Besides, the NBA was changing and certain old-school style of play no longer worked as effectively as they did before. Kobe showed that he was adaptable and changed his game. He combined relentless offense with intense defense which made himself a lethal weapon. He didn't care if he wasn't the strongest nor the fastest because he knew that the only way to sustain his longevity and success is through adaptability.

1. Success is the equilibrium point where preparation meets opportunity.

Kobe's work ethic is unparalleled. At a young age, he was already preparing himself for the NBA. He didn't know when opportunities would strike so he kept himself in excellent game shape. Prep work is extremely important to Kobe because it gave him the edge. It allowed him to be two steps ahead of his opponents. He made himself physically and mentally conditioned so that when great opportunities came, he was ready to rise to the occasion.

Conclusion

I'd like to thank you and congratulate you for transiting my lines from start to finish.

I hope this book was able to help you understand and appreciate Kobe Bryant beyond the realm of basketball. While it's true that his life revolved around basketball, his legacy encompassed his off-court brilliance. The life that he leads now is the culmination of all the hard work spanning over two decades. His journey to *legendhood* was not always smooth sailing. In fact, it was rough and turbulent. At times, it seemed that everyone wanted him to fail, but failing was never an option for the Black Mamba.

Kobe's life is a story of a never-ending quest to improve his life. As the world around him changed, he adapted and thrived. He kept reinventing himself not just to stay relevant, but to always be the best version of himself.

If you are inspired by Kobe's remarkable resilience and toughness, the next step is to pursue something that you are passionate about and develop a winning mentality to achieve your dreams and make a positive impact.

I wish you the best of luck!

Patrick Thompson

CPSIA information can be obtained
at www.ICGtesting.com
Printed in the USA
LVHW082154300120
645415LV00017B/918